HOW TO DESIGN A TEACHING SYLLABUS

ISBN 978-1-4092-0323-0

INDEX

Introduction....4

Legal Framework....6

Context....9

Syllabus designed related to the official curriculum....12

Course adaptation....18

Methodology....30

Attention to students with special needs of educational support. Catering for diversity....40

Assessment....43

Structure of the teaching units....50

1. INTRODUCTION.

1.1. Importance of planning.

What we do in class with our students is the result of many decisions which have been debated and defined before the class itself. On the one hand, we have to take into account that we have to make many spontaneous decisions when we are face to face with our pupils. On other, we have to make adjustments to our lesson plans as we go along with the classes as a result of the many circumstances we may find within the class. However, we cannot forget that education is systematic, intentional and planned, in contrast to other types of learning.

As you probably assume, assembling a syllabus or teaching plan is one of the essential activities of a teacher's work. In this specific case, the syllabus is designed for the 1st year of *Bacharelato* (Non-compulsory Secondary Education)

In any case, we should start by asking ourselves: What does planning or programming means? A teaching plan implies designing the activities to be carried out, ordered in a sequence and with a specific time allocation, in order to achieve certain objectives, and being able to rely on appropriate teaching materials and resources.

A syllabus could be defined as the planning of ordered and sequenced teaching units, designed and developed in each subject for a specific level.

Teacher planning is built from curricula that guide towards certain objectives by means of activities derived from the content to be taught. To this end, there are certain assessment criteria applying to the mentioned activities which will indicate the level of achievement of those objectives.

Teacher planning is part of an attempt at rationalizing teaching practice in order to have it follow a pre-determined plan and leaves as little as possible to chance. One of the features of teacher programming is putting teaching activity in context with the aim of planning in the most realistic way possible and gaining a greater knowledge of the environment in which the teaching/learning process will take place.

The syllabuses for each subject will aim at guaranteeing both horizontal coordination (among the subjects making up each course), and vertical sequencing in the treatment of a given area of learning throughout the several years of the stage.

1.2. Importance of English in the general development of the secondary education student.

The learning of foreign languages contributes both to the fostering of a well-rounded personality and to social integration. Moreover, knowledge of foreign languages is seen as a necessity in modern society. The intensification of international relations, the increased opportunities of working abroad, the influence of foreign languages on the media and the extensive use of new technologies makes it necessary to enlarge our knowledge of foreign languages in order to become integrated in the present society. In particular, knowledge of foreign languages is regarded as an essential tool that enables people to have free movement within the European Union and that contributes to the promotion of cultural, economic and technical ties

THE COUNCIL OF EUROPE. THE PORTFOLIO. Due to the political importance given to the learning of foreign languages, the Council of Europe has produced a reference document for teachers and textbook writers which can help us to decide what to teach in class, to elaborate language syllabuses, examinations, etc., so that a degree obtained in one country can be recognized and accepted in another. This reference document is known as **CEF** or **Common European Framework**, and part of the document sets out "reference levels" as a way of describing someone's ability in the language. There are six basic reference levels: A1, A2, B1, B2, C1 and C2. Level A1 corresponds to a basic user of the language, and C2 to a proficient user. The CEF also recommends that students use a **Portfolio** (a document that aims to help students reflect on, record and demonstrate their language learning).

2. LEGAL FRAMEWORK.

It is well-known fact that these are times of transition for the Spanish Educational System. On the one hand, the *Organic Law on Education (LOE)* was passed in April 2006, and came into effect twenty days after its publication in the *BOE* (Official State Bulletin). The calendar for the application of that law is featured in the *Royal Decree 806/2006, June 30th;* therefore, the law wull be gradually developed and applied throughout the next few terms. It is for this reason that, for the purposes of the present program, we will be considering many aspects of the former *Organic Law on the General Organization of the Educational System (Ley Orgánica General del Sistema Educativo* or *LOGSE), October 1990* and of the *Organic Law on the Quality of Education (Ley Orgánica de*

Calidad de la Educación or *LOCE), December 2002*. According to paragraph 3 of section B.1) in point 9.5, *"programs will consist of the curricula published in the DOGA at the time of publication of the examination session."*

To summarize, we could say that the components of this syllabus are based on the laws now applicable, but with an eye on the developments of the present education system, which are to have an influence on future planning.

<u>Specific list of the legislation considered for the development of this syllabus:</u>

ORGANIC LAWS.

- *Organic Law 1/1990, October 3rd, on the General Organization of the Educational System.*
- *Organic Law 10/2002, December 23rd, on the Quality of Education.*
- *Organic Law 2/2006, May 3rd, on Education.*

CURRICULUM.

- *Royal Decree 3474/2000, December 29th, by which the minimal teaching contents of Bacharelato are established.*
- *Decree 231/2002, June 6th, which establishes the curriculum for Bacharelato in the Autonomous Community of Galicia and which modifies the Decree 275/1994, July 29th, by which the curriculum for Bacharelato in the Autonomous Community of Galicia is established.*

- *Decree 275/1994, July 29th, by which the curriculum for Bacharelato in the Autonomous Community of Galicia is established.*

ASSESSMENT.

- *Order ECD/1923/2003, July 8th, which establishes the basic elements of the assessment documents of General Education regulated by the Organic Law 10/2002, December 23rd, on the Quality of Education, as well as the formal requirements derived from the assessment process which are necessary to guarantee student mobility.*
- *Error Correction of the Order ECD/1993/2003, July 8th.*

MINIMAL REQUIREMENTS OF SCHOOLS.

- *Royal Decree 1537/2003, December 5th, by which the minimal requirements of schools that teach general education are established.*

Other legislative dispositions exist that affect our syllabus (such as those concerning specific educational needs), and they will be explained in detail at appropriate moments and will be cited in the legislative bibliography.

3. CONTEXT.

One of the conditioning factors when putting together a syllabus is the adequacy of the curriculum to the actual circumstances of the school where our subject is to be taught. A teaching plan must be realistic, will be developed on the basis of a legal framework, and will be designed for a school within a specific context and for a group of students with a set of known circumstances (environment, family, school history, etc.).

3.1. The school to which this syllabus will be applied.

The LOE, in chapter II of title V, refers to school autonomy, and specifies that schools will have the right to shape, approve and implement education and management projects (still to be developed). The *PEC (Proxecto Educativo do Centro* or School Educational Project) states that schools are to reflect the values, objectives and priorities of action; also, that they are to adopt specifications to the curricula (present PCC) and the transversal area treatment.

Our school's Educational Project reflects environment-related aspects such as:

a) Sociological and geographical factors: The school where the classroom plan is to be implemented is a prototypical secondary school in a small country town in Galicia, a largely rural area with a recent increase in the number of pupils from other cultural backgrounds. Because of its location, we can find different kinds of students, stemming from high, mid or low-class families. This diversity enriches students by putting them in touch with different social classes. We must remark that this school, since it takes in students not only from the town but also from nearby villages, provides buses which transport students to and from school. In addition, this centre provides schooling for 617 students.

b) Material means and facilities: The high school meets the minimal requirements of schools that teach general education (as stated in the *Royal Decree 1537/2003, December 5th*). Moreover, we can remark that the school is house in fully-equipped, modern buildings which are provided with the most up-to-date materials and didactic resources.

c) These are the educational levels available at the school:

**ESO* (Compulsory Secondary Education): 16 ESO units.

**Bacharelato* (Non-compulsory Secondary Education): 6 *Bacharelato* units. The students of *Bacharelato* can follow Science and Technological, Humanities and Social Sciences options.

3.2. General description of students at this stage.

As mentioned before, this syllabus has been designed for the level of 1st year of *Bacharelato*. According to the *LOE*, chapter IV, article 32, *Bacharelato* consists of two courses, it being possible for this stage to take up to four courses under ordinary circumstances. In such conditions, students of *Bacharelato* will generally be between the ages of 16 and 20. This will influence strategies of action regarding students and, therefore, teacher planning.

Although at these ages they have already undergone the great physical changes of adolescence, students are still experiencing emotional and social changes of great importance, mainly affecting three types of development:

-Cognitive development. Progress related to rational and intellectual components.

-Social development. The progress of acquiring skills that makes one become an active member of society.

-Moral development. Acquiring behaviour on the basis of values, rules, customs and regulations accepted in one's social environment.

They are at that age in which they are still receiving information from the world so as to form their opinions on relevant issues. Moreover, they are at a stage in which they have to start making choices which will determine their future. Intellectually, they are more mature and have developed their abstract reasoning. They are more independent and in most cases they are ready to start assuming responsibility for their own learning.

3.3. Group of students which are the object of this syllabus.

Since we do not know beforehand the specific features of the students this syllabus is aimed at, the strategies will be generic. However, we will not rule out the presence of some student with serious learning deficiencies.

It is in fact quite probable that in the group of students, which are the object of this syllabus there will be some with difficulties related to learning disabilities, which may affect performance in the subject at hand.

The condition of having passed *ESO* acts as an important filter for the profile of the students gaining access to *Bacharelato*. even so, it is likely that in our group of reference there will be students requiring personalized treatment due to a variety of causes (highly gifted or hyperactive students, students with problematic behaviours or a lower level of knowledge than is required, etc.). It will therefore be necessary to respond to students with special educational needs, as reflected in the applicable legislation

4. SYLLABUS DESIGN RELATED TO THE OFFICIAL CURRICULUM.

4.1. AIMS OF THE *BACHARELATO* STAGE.

The *Bacharelato* goals, expressed in the Article 25 of the *LOGSE* are the following:

Bacharelato will provide students with an intellectual and humane maturity, as well as with the knowledge and skills which will permit them to develop their social functions responsibly and competitively. Likewise, it will prepare them to gain access to High Level Vocational Training and university studies.

4.2. GENERAL AIMS FOR THE *BACHARELATO* STAGE.

They refer to what we intend students to develop as a result of the education they receive; objectives, therefore, establish the skills or levels of competence the students are expected to reach.

According to Art. 25 of *Decree 275/1994, Bacharelato has the aim of developing the following abilities in the pupils:*

a) To master Spanish and Galician language.

b) To be able to express themselves fluently and correctly in a foreign language.

c) To be able to critically analyze and assess the realities of the contemporary world and those events and factors that influence it.

d) To be able to understand the fundamental elements of scientific research and method.

e) To consolidate a personal, social and moral maturity which will permit them to act in a responsible and autonomous way.

f) To participate with a sense of solidarity in the development and improvement of their social environment.

g) To master the fundamental aspects of scientific and technological knowledge, and the basic skills corresponding to the option chosen.

h) To develop an artistic and literary sensitivity as a source of educational and cultural enrichment.

4.3. GENERAL AIMS FOR FOREIGN LANGUAGE LEARNING IN *BACHARELATO*.

The *Decree 231/2002*, June 6th, establishes the following objectives for the subject of Foreign Language Learning (in this case, English) for the stage of *Bacharelato*:

***a) To use the foreign language orally and in writing in order to communicate fluently and correctly by means of the use of appropriate strategies*.**

At the *Bacharelato* stage, oral skills are expected to be fluent. Students are expected to modify and adapt their language to the context in which the language is used, taking into account the setting, participants, topic... Therefore, students participate in communication situations which, in many cases, allow them to practise freely. As for written expression, it should respond to the criteria of accuracy, taking into account the different types of text the students will be working with.

b) To understand and critically interpret oral, written and visual texts from everyday communicative situations and from the media

Students will be working with semi-authentic and authentic material and will interpret verbal and non-verbal information. This gives students a taste of "real" language in use, and provides them with valid linguistic data for their unconscious acquisition processes to work on. The learning process may be as similar as possible to the acquisition of their mother tongue.

***c) To read general texts or texts related to students' interests by themselves, to understand their essential elements and to grasp their function and discursive organization*.**

Students will work with different text types (descriptions, formal and informal letters, reviews, etc.) dealing with modern-day topics. This will help them see reading as a source of information and as a pleasure.

d) To use comprehension strategies which allow the meaning of unfamiliar words to be inferred from context, from their own knowledge of the world, and from socio-linguistic aspects such as word-formation, prefixes and suffixes, synonyms and antonyms, etc.

Pupils need to be helped to become good readers, identifying and putting into practice various comprehension strategies. It should be taken into account that good readers use their imagination and previous experience to help them understand a text, and are critical and independent, being able to infer meaning from context without always relying on dictionaries.

e) To reflect on the functioning of the foreign language in communication, with the aim of improving the student's own production and his or her understanding of others in increasingly varied and unpredictable situations.

Contents which were previously dealt with in isolation at earlier stages are now treated in an integrated manner in order to establish comparisons and links between them. In the proposed tasks, students observe and analyze data, draw conclusions and apply them. Only by doing this will students achieve communicative competence.

f) To reflect on one's own learning process by using one's own resources based on observation, correction and evaluation with a view to knowing at all times one's own stage and to continuing the study of the foreign language in the future.

At the *Bacharelato* level it is important that students take responsibility of their own learning process, developing individual learning styles, depending on their interests and future needs. This development of autonomy and "learning to learn" strategies will be useful in various fields of knowledge.

g) To reflect on how languages work, by establishing parallelisms and contrast between known languages and the foreign language.

The students must be aware of the historical links between languages and, thus, exploit the similarities between them. On the other hand, they must also be aware of differences (e.g. "false friends).

h) To develop imagination, sensitivity and creativity in the use and the learning of the foreign language.

Throughout the year, we will be continuously working on these abilities by letting students produce their own pieces of writing in English as well as by using authentic and dynamic material which will provide them with significant learning.

i) To appreciate the value of the foreign language as a means of gaining access to other information and cultures, thus rendering the comprehension of our own language and culture easier.

Throughout various didactic units we will be showing similarities and differences between the culture of Anglo-Saxon speaking countries and Galician culture. We will demonstrate that some similarities do exist between both cultures (e.g. *Halloween* and *Samaín*) and thus build a bridge between them.

j) To get to know about the fundamental aspects of the socio-cultural environment of the foreign language in order to achieve a better level of communication and of interpretation of cultures different from one's own, in the search for better international understanding.

When learning a foreign language it is important to develop a socio-cultural competence which will allow students to use language appropriately taking into account the value and culture associated to that language. All the text contain implicit socio-cultural references which the student must interpret and apply to their own production of the target language.

k) To critically evaluate other ways of organizing experience and structuring personal relations by understanding the relative value of cultural norms and conventions.

Mastering a foreign language represents a way of improving relations between different peoples, and sharing experiences with other people. Students are encouraged to become aware that cultural norms and conventions have a relative value.

l) To reflect about the similarities and differences between the various cultures and develop tolerance for them, in the search for a higher level of tolerance between peoples.

Students have to become respectful and tolerant of cultures different to their own. Their experience will be enriched by contact with texts that greatly reflect socio-cultural elements.

5. COURSE ADAPTATION.

We can define "course adaptation" as a demarcation within the syllabus, of those aspects which only concern an academic year, in this case, the 1st year of *Bacharelato* (Non-compulsory Secondary Education).

5.1. SPECIFIC AIMS FOR FOREIGN LANGUAGE LEARNING IN THE 1ST YEAR OF *BACHARELATO.*

Specific aims are the goals we intend our students to achieve at the end of the course and they constitute the immediate point of reference for the assessment of the processes and results of the learning of our students.

The aims to be met for Foreign Language Learning (in this case, English) in the 1st year of *Bacharelato* are the following:

******Communicative skills.**

a) To comprehend global and specific information in oral messages, written and visual texts.

b) To recognize the communicative strategies used by speakers and in authentic written texts on subjects of general interest.

c) To use skills and strategies appropriate for different text types and reading purposes.

d) To take part in conversations or discussions prepared beforehand, using appropriate strategies to ensure effective communication.

e) To produce coherent messages with enough accuracy to make communication possible.

f) Understand the essential information in different texts on up-to-date topics, on the socio-cultural reality of English-speaking countries or in informative texts, predicting and inferring data by using context.

g) To write different texts which are sufficiently accurate grammatically while, at the same time, using the diverse elements which give cohesion and coherence to a text.

****Reflection on language.**

a) To reflect on how a language works through inductive and deductive learning of its grammar rules.

b) To use linguistic reference items (grammatical, lexical, orthographic, phonetic and textual) to facilitate systematic learning.

c) To apply grammatical knowledge to new situations.

d) To use resources, sources of information and reference material autonomously to draw conclusions, to consolidate knowledge systematically.

e) To reflect one's own learning process in order to reformulate rules, to define what has been learnt and to advance in the learning process.

****Socio-cultural aspects.**

a) To interpret cultural elements of English-speaking countries.

b) To show knowledge of geographical, historical, artistic, literary aspects of English-speaking countries by incorporating this knowledge into contextualized communicative situations.

c) To show proximity to the social and cultural diversity transmitted when communicating in the foreign language, and look for similarities and differences.

d) To show interest in valuing positively the use of English as a means of international communication.

e) To understand and appreciate the use of English in the field of technology.

f) To get to know one's own culture better through the study of socio-cultural aspects transmitted by the foreign language.

5.2. CONTENTS FOR ENGLISH IN THE 1st YEAR OF *BACHARELATO*.

Contents are those curricular elements whose knowledge is considered to be especially relevant for fostering and strengthening the all-round development of the students.

Following the *Decree 231/2002, June 6th*, the contents for English in the 1st year of *Bacharelato* have been grouped into three categories:

I. Communicative skills.

- Extraction of global and specific information from oral and written texts with some specific aims: identification of main ideas, checking of previous data, giving opinion about the ideas of the text, discussing…

-Prediction and deduction of information in different text types and consequent verification of the ideas or suppositions brought forward by means of a subsequent listening or reading.

-Comprehensive listening of messages delivered by speakers with different accents.

-Oral interaction with other people, by planning beforehand the message to be delivered or the information to be required, and by taking care over coherence as well as over formal correctness.

-Descriptions and narrations based on personal experiences or opinions.

-Formulation of hypotheses on the expectations, interests or communicative attitudes of the texts' addressees.

-Logical order of sentences and paragraphs so as to produce a coherent text, by using appropriate linking items.

-Writing of various text types (narrative texts, descriptive texts, letters, summaries, projects…), both formal and informal, by respecting their structure.

II. Reflection on language.

II.1. Language and grammatical functions.

II.1.a. *Describing physical appearance, state of health, character, likings and interests. Comparing, making contrasts and distinguishing between data and opinions. Expressing preferences.*

-Present Simple/Present Continuous.

-Like/enjoy/love/hate/prefer…+ gerund (-ing) or to + infinitive.

-Stative verbs: believe, know, seem…

-Adjectives. Comparative and superlative.

-Phrasal verbs to express physical features.

-Relative pronouns.

-Defining and non-defining relative clauses.

II.1.b. *Talking about habits in the past. Expressing the changes produced in those changes and in surrounding things.*

-Past Simple/Past Continuous.

-Present Perfect + just/yet/already.

-For/since/ago/during.

-Past Perfect.

-Passive Voice.

-Would/used to + infinitive.

-Could/was able to…

-Be/get used to + ing.

-Uses of gerund after prepositions and as a subject.

-Manner and degree adverbs.

II.1.c. *Expressing plans and arrangements with various time references. Arranging appointments. Predicting events and forecasting.*

-Present Continuous/Will/Be going to. Review of differences.

-When/as soon as/before/after…+ Present Simple.

-When/as soon as/before/after…+ Present Perfect.

-Future Progressive.

II.1.d. *Expressing obligation and absence of obligation, necessity, ability, possibility, prohibition, asking for and giving permission or advice.*

-Must/mustn't

-Should/ought to

-Need/needn't

-Have to/don't have to

-Can/be able to/could

-Can/could/may.

***II.1.e.** Expressing real possibility and formulating hypotheses.*

-Conditional sentences type I, II and III.

-Use of "unless".

***II.1.f.** Reporting what someone else has said, asked, ordered or suggested.*

-Reported speech: questions, declarative sentences, orders and suggestions.

-Reporting verbs: ask, declare, apologise, explain, invite, offer, say, suggest, tell…

***II.1.g.** Making deductions, suppositions or references to present and past actions.*

-Must, can, may, could, should + infinitive.

-Must, can, may, could, should + perfect infinitive.

***II.1.h.** Expressing consequence, result and cause.*

-Subordinate clauses introduced by the connectives: because, since, so as, as a result, consequently, etc…

-Have/get + something + Past Participiple.

II. 2. Vocabulary and Semantics.

-Vocabulary related to the topics dealt with: personal experiences, pieces of news, leisure (sports, trips, holidays), interests, places, physical appearance, health, family friendships relations, new technologies, science, etc…

-Formulae and expressions.

II.3. Phonetics.

-Pronunciation of vowel and consonant phonemes as well as difficult diphthongs: mute sounds, semivowels, semiconsonants, etc…

-Pronunciation of weak forms: have/has/was/were, etc…

-Word and sentence stress.

-Sentence intonation.

-Rhythm.

III. Socio-cultural aspects.

-Positive evaluation of the use of the foreign language as a means of overcoming understanding and communication barriers between peoples.

-Contrast between daily cultural aspects transmitted by the foreign language and those transmitted by one's culture: family traditions, sports, educational system, etc....

-Adaptation of messages to each interlocutor's characteristics.

-Identification of traditions and daily features of the culture of English-speaking countries: Time, celebrations, etc...

-Use of linguistic formulae appropriate for each communicative situation: greetings and farewells, polite requests, etc...

-Realization of the presence and importance of the foreign language in information and communication new technologies.

IV. Attitudes, values and rules.

-Using a discourse appropriate to the different communicative situations.

-Critically evaluating the information received in the foreign language.

-Becoming interested in using language in a creative way.

-Valuing the importance of socio-linguistic conventions in speech acts in the foreign language.

-Using the foreign language as a means of gaining access to information about the different subjects of the curriculum.

-Appreciating the personal or professional enrichment provided by the knowledge of several languages.

-Reflecting on how languages work, from the similarities and differences established between their linguistic systems.

-Valuing the knowledge of a foreign language as a means of access and communication among peoples and other cultures; as well as its presence in the use of new technologies.

-Appreciating the differences among diverse cultures and showing a tolerant and respective attitude towards them.

5.3. TRANSVERSAL TOPICS.

As teachers, we have to take into account that, apart from the information content of any unit (the subject matter which the language is used to express) and the language component itself (grammar, pronunciation...), any material we present to our students transmits ideas and values, and that our job as teachers is not only to teach language but also to educate our pupils, forming their attitudes and moral values, to help them become responsible citizens who make a positive contribution to society. I want my pupils to develop moral values and attitudes through awareness and experience, so I want to provide opportunities to gain that awareness and experience in the classroom through the materials and activities I will be using. Listening and reading are a source of information for students, so by providing listening and reading material which contains examples of the moral values and attitudes we want to transmit, we will be educating them and making them aware of their rights and duties as citizens in our society. The transversal topics cover areas of awareness or social consciousness and provide a valuable source for the development of moral attitudes.

According to article 96, “g” section of the Organic Regulations for secondary education schools, the teaching program must include the programming of transversal subjects. Also, article 121 of the LOE states that the PEC must include, among other documents, the document dealing with transversal treatment of areas.

As is well known, the basic purpose of school education is to contribute to the development of individuals who are well equipped for life within society. Contemporary world conflicts in the form of violence, inequality, the lack of moral values, squandered resources, a degraded environment, or habits which are a danger to health cannot be overlooked by the educational system (Ministry of Education and Science, 1993).

The inclusion of transversal subjects among areas aims at making up for certain social needs inherited from a traditional culture, in an attempt to transform them by means of an education based on values. Next follows a summary of the treatment of these contents and their particular inclusion in the teaching units.

- **Education for peace.** Reflection and debates related to an education for peace may be introduced by means of specific subjects, such as the history of aviation or artificial satellites.
- **Consumer education.** This may be treated along with content related to object analysis at the sociological level, advertising, etc.
- **Environmental education.** Contents related to the environment are reflected in the study of environmental conditioning and the different varieties of matter.

- **Health education.** This subject is subsumed within the study of security and hygiene in the workplace.
- **Education for equality.** Education for equal opportunity for both sexes finds expression in sharing tasks among the different groups in a non-discriminatory fashion.
- **Civic and moral education.** This is treated along with contents related to the field of work, as well as the social and environmental impact of technological products and processes.

6. METHODOLOGY.

The final objective in the teaching of a foreign language is achieving **communicative competence** in that language, that is, being able to use the language appropriately depending on who we are talking to, why we are talking, or what we are talking about. Thus, we will adopt a **communicative approach.** In recent years, a number of reasons have contributed to the importance of the communicative approaches to foreign language teaching. Nowadays, it is generally recognized that traditional methods based exclusively on grammar did not meet the demands of today's learners.

Now, what is the main feature of the communicative approach? It is an eclectic approach that focuses on the **use of language** rather than on the analysis of its structure. It is widely accepted that the internalization of rules which generate sentences is more important than the mechanical memorization of endless and often meaningless lists of phrases and structures.

A communicative approach to teaching a foreign language also requires attention to the following issues:

6.1. THE ROLE OF THE TEACHER.

While the increasing emphasis on student autonomy in education has moved the centre of gravity away from the teacher and closer to the student, the teacher continues to have a key role in student learning. A good teacher can be defined as a teacher who helps the student to learn. He or she contributes to this in a number of ways. The role of the teacher in the classroom depends on the nature of activity developed:

a) The teacher may be a **facilitator** or manager of the students' learning: he/she provides resources, monitors progress and encourages students to problem-solve.

b) The teacher may be an **organizer:** Since teaching is the organization of learning, a teacher must essentially be an organizer. The task of any organizer is to enable a group and the individuals in it to function effectively together for the achievement of a common purpose.

c) The teacher may act as an **assessor**: The assessment of the student's competence is one of the most important tasks facing the teacher.

6.2. TREATMENT OF ERROR.

One of the main dilemmas for teachers is error correction. It is always tricky to know when and if to correct students and how to go about it. The danger of over-correcting is that students will lose motivation and we may even destroy the flow of the class or the activity by butting in and correcting every single mistake. The other extreme is to let the conversation flow and not to correct any mistakes. There are times when this is appropriate but most students want to have some of their mistakes corrected as it gives them a basis for improvement, as the classic saying goes *"you always learn from your mistakes"*.

Concerning this topic, we can reach the conclusion that in the **communicative approach**, the achievement of spontaneous communication and fluency becomes the main objective, even at the expense of grammatical correctness and accuracy. Errors and mistakes are considered as a normal and even positive part of the learning process.

Related to this is the concept of "**interlanguage"**, seen as the linguistic system that a learner constructs on his way to the mastery of a target language, that is, an intermediate status between his native language and the target language.

6.3. THE ROLE OF THE LEARNER.

In the communicative approach learners should take on **more active roles** in the classroom. An emphasis is put on significant learning, that is, on meaningful and useful stretches of language used in context, which will increase pupils' motivation to study the foreign language.

Here we will follow Ausubel's Theory of Meaningful Learning. He states that the student's learning depends on his/her previous cognitive structure (that is, the collection of ideas and concepts an individual has about a specific field of knowledge and its organization) that gets connected, in the first place, with the new information acquired and also with other subjects (what we call "interdisciplinarity") and with his/her own life. Throughout these connections, learning becomes meaningful since it turns out to be interesting to the student.

But there is another important aspect of the learner's role which takes place outside the classroom: learner autonomy. "Learning to learn" strategies must be developed, so that students may become autonomous learners, willing to take risks with the new language, making hypotheses on the appropriate form and function of structures after observing use in context.

6.4. CONCEPT OF "TASK".

A task is defined as any purposeful action considered by an individual as necessary in order to achieve a given result in the context of an objective to be achieved. Task-based syllabuses represent a particular realization of communicative language teaching. They are based on the belief that students may learn more effectively when their minds are focused on the target tasks they need to carry out in the "real world" outside the classroom, rather than on the language they are using. Examples of target tasks include taking part in a job interview or finding one's way from a hotel to a subway station.

6.5. INTEGRATING THE FOUR SKILLS.

By organizing our classroom around practical tasks that learners will use "in the real world", we will integrate reading, speaking, listening and writing in various ways and combinations in ways that are natural and self-reinforcing.

Listening, speaking, reading and writing are means of communication and among them, listening and reading are considered as receptive skills that help students get information as the input of language, whereas speaking and writing are both treated as productive skills that make language output possible and require sufficient language input as their basis.

Integrating the four skills emphasizes the focus on realistic language and can therefore lead to the students' all-round development of communicative competence in English. Moreover, there are other reasons why integration can benefit a communicative classroom. Firstly, integrating the skills allows a teacher to build in more variety into the lesson because the range of activities will be wider. Secondly, integration of skills satisfies the students' different learning styles in that the extroverts may speak a lot, the introverts prefer to listen or read, and the analytically or visually oriented learners like to see how words are written and sentences constructed.

6.6. TEACHING/LEARNING ACTIVITIES.

Planning of activities requires previous analysis and consideration of what we intend to develop, what the objective is and at what point activities should be introduced.

For the choice of activities the following criteria have been considered:

- That they develop the skill for the objective we are pursuing.

- That they be significant and suitable for the global development of the group.

- That they be versatile and combine concepts, procedures and attitudes.

- That they be sequenced according to their difficulty and follow process continuity.

- That they require a cognitive effort to complete them successfully.

- If possible, that the student take part in the choice of activities.

Classification of activities according to their purpose

Initial activities / Previous knowledge activities: performed in order to know the ideas, opinions, or possible misconceptions that may impede the teaching/learning process.

Introduction / motivation activities: with these we try to interest the student in the contents dealt with and to apply the theoretical part that has been explained. Their purpose is to "hook" the student. They should be easy and original.

Development activities: in these, the concepts, procedures and attitudes of the teaching unit are worked upon so as to develop the corresponding skills and capacities.

Consolidation activities: new ideas are contrasted with the previous ones in order to create a new perspective with a cognitive impact aimed at strengthening the new structures.

Enforcement / Support activities: As a measure to cater to diversity, for each teaching unit, educational support activities have been devised for students in need of strengthening mainly their concepts and procedures. These support activities are aimed at reaching the required minimum objectives.

Widening activities: For each teaching unit some extension activity has been established with a view to help those students showing an interest above the average, specific motivation in dealing with a given subject or a greater capacity. What is intended with these activities is to relate concepts and extend contents that may pose a challenge and allow the student to progress along the teaching/learning process.

Assessment activities / Progress checks: even though assessment of the teaching/learning process is continuous, it is advisable to propose a series of more complete" activities that relate various concepts and are useful to assess the degree of success regarding objectives.

6.7. STUDENT GROUPING.

In this section we will allude to grouping for the performance of activities during teaching units.

It is a well-known fact that group techniques are conducive to socialization, foster an attitude of co-operative responsibility, achieve a wider set of objectives in both the cognitive and emotional spheres, provide the opportunity to compare points of view, strengthen critical spirit, etc. However, this is not an easily applicable technique, generally due to the excessively large number of students, static or cluttered desks, lack of space, the time available for organizing the classroom, etc.

We will indicate the different work modes to be applied in our classroom: IA (individual activity), SGA (small group activity: pairs, threes...), GGA (large group or class group activity). The explanation of contents by the teacher is specified as T/L A (teaching/learning activity). If any of the activities is to be done at home, it appears indicated as HA.

Even so, the present syllabus has tried to apply this methodology in at least one session of each teaching unit, which I justify by enumerating a series of advantages:

- It is an active methodology, since attention focuses on the group, not on the teacher.

- It is an empirical methodology, founded on the development of personal experience.

- It is a critical methodology, since it is conducive to reflection, respect for ideas, contrasting opinions, etc.

- It is a methodology that involves analysis, of both content and process.

- It is a communicative methodology which fosters interpersonal communication, where the student is both addresser and addressee.

General criteria employed in forming work groups:

- At the beginning of the course I have followed the "proximity" criterion.

- As one becomes acquainted with the students, they should be grouped so as to favour integration, for example combining more communicative students with shy students.

- Groups shall be heterogeneous regarding capacity, gender, race, motivation, etc.

- The tendency will be to group students with learning difficulties with the best performers which have a cooperative attitude.

6.8. MATERIAL RESOURCES.

Resources are "anything which can be used to facilitate the learning of a language". We can divide these material resources according to their physical support:

(a) Traditional means (various sorts of boards, print resources, books, magazines, newspapers, brochures, OHPs...).

(b) Audiovisual means (Radio, TV, CDs, DVDs...)

(c) New Technologies (Programs, Internet resources -webquests, chat rooms, blogs…-).

LIST OF RECOMMENDED WEB PAGES:

www.bbc.co.uk/learningenglish
http://www.eslcafe.com/idea/index.cgi

http://www.manythings.org

http://www.saberingles.com.ar/index.html

http://a4esl.org/

http://esl.about.com/

http://www.dailyesl.com/

http://www.elllo.org/

http://www.englishclub.com/

7. ATTENTION TO STUDENTS WITH SPECIAL NEEDS OF EDUCATIONAL SUPPORT. CATERING FOR DIVERSITY.

Differences between individuals constitute an inescapable fact that conditions the entire teaching/learning process. Students indeed differ in the rate of their progress, their learning style, previous knowledge, experiences, circumstances and environment, capacities… All of this makes it necessary for teachers to educate for diversity.

Among the various conditions that can and usually do mark the diversity of our students we can find: **(a)** students with a different level of curricular competence, **(b)** students that find themselves in different moments of psychological development, **(c)** students with various motivations and interests, **(d)** students with different learning styles, and **(e)** students from diverse socio-cultural backgrounds.

The *Article 71* in the *LOE* establishes that *the Educational Authorities will guarantee the appropriate resources so that students who require educational attention different from the ordinary one (…) can reach the the maximum development of their personal capacities and, in any case, the objectives established in a general way for all students.*

Within this great diversity, only some students will require **Specific Needs of Educational Support (*NEAE*).** That is why we should not mix "Catering for diversity" with "Specific Needs of Educational Support". Within the latter term (coined by the *LOE*) we can include:

- **Highly gifted students** (who will be either all-round gifted students or just have a higher English level than the other students). With the aim of offering a more suitable educational solution for these students, necessary measures will be taken to identify and evaluate at an early stage their needs. Regarding this subject, the *Royal Decree 943/2003, July 18th*, and the *Order from October 28th, 1996* must be mentioned by which the conditions to make more flexible the length of the different levels and stages of the educational system for intellectually gifted students are regulated.

- **Students who have been incorporated at a late stage into the Spanish educational system**. According to the *Order from February 20th, 2004*, incorporation to the educational system will favour students from other countries, especially those in the age of compulsory education. For students that do not know Spanish language and culture, or who present serious gaps in basic knowledge, specific learning programs will be designed with the aim of easing their integration of these students in the corresponding levels.
- **Students with any kind of special educational need**. Whatever the case, according to the *Decree 320/1996, July 26th*, and the *Order from December 27th, 2002*, those students with any kind of special need should be schooled, as a general rule, in ordinary centres.

There are some principles that must be applied when dealing with students with some kind of educational need:

a) **Standardization** in the treatment of disabled people.

b) **Sectorization** of services for handicapped people.

c) **Inclusion** of disabled people into the ordinary schooling.

d) **Individualization** of the teaching/learning process.

Next, I would like to talk about the various measures which should be taken to cater for the different needs of students. According to the *Order from October 6th, 1995*, the official curriculum can be modified in every element to cater for diversity.

Among ordinary measures, we can mention **Educational Reinforcement** For each teaching unit, educational support activities have been devised for students in need of strengthening mainly their concepts and procedures. These support activities are aimed at reaching the required minimum objectives of the course. Also proposed for such students is specific grouping with good performers who are especially receptive, who can serve as a model and guide for specific activities.

On the other hand, for each teaching unit, some expansion activities have been established with a view to help those students showing an interest above the average, specific motivation in dealing with a given subject or a greater capacity.

Another measure is the choice of **elective subjects**, which favours the individualization of the curriculum, according to the capacities and educational needs of each student.

Any measure of catering for diversity exceeding ordinary measures should be undertaken on the basis of diagnosis, advice and follow-up by the Counselling Department. For instance, **Curricular Adaptation**, which affects prescriptive elements of the curriculum (objectives, contents and assessment criteria), is rare in *Bacharelato*, although we could find a **Curricular Adaptation of resources** (e.g. for a visually-handicapped student).

8. ASSESSMENT

Assessment is an essential part of teaching tasks. First of all, we must ask ourselves what the term "assessment" means. It could be defined as a rigorous and systematic process of gathering and analysis of information, through various procedures and instruments, of all the elements of the T/L process.

I would like to remark that any kind of assessment should serve as a form of assistance for our students, not as a form of censorship or punishment. Assessment has various aims: **(a)** It gives us clues about how well our students are performing their tasks, and about any problems they may have; **(b)** it also gives us clues about how effective our teaching is, in case we need to change some aspects; **(c)** it gives students a reference about their progress and may make them feel more confident in that they know they are learning.

Here the *Order ECD/1923/2003, July 8th*, must be mentioned, *which establishes the basic elements of the assessment documents of General Education regulated by the Organic Law 10/2002, December 23rd, on the Quality of Education, as well as the formal requirements derived from the assessment process which are necessary to guarantee student mobility* and also the *Error Correction of the Order ECD/1993/2003, July 8th*.

Assessment at this stage should be identified by the following features:

- It must be **global**. We do not only evaluate students, but also ourselves (teachers) and our syllabus.
- It must be **continuous**. We are looking at assessment as an integral part of the teaching and learning process, aimed at detecting difficulties as soon as they arise, finding out their causes, and, consequently, adapting teaching and learning activities by establishing remedial exams.
- It must **integrate**. The integrative character of assessment in *Bacharelato* demands taking into account the

general skills established in the stage objectives by way of the skills required for the objectives of the different areas and subjects.

- It must be **formative, qualitative and contextualized**. Assessment will be linked to its environment and to a specific process of teaching and learning, so that it will provide continuous and significant information for both teachers and students.

Assessing our students...

WHAT TO ASSESS?

When taking about "what to assess" we must take into consideration the **assessment criteria**. One of the aims of assessment is to determine the degree of attainment of the proposed objectives. That is the reason why we must define some criteria that can be observed and measured throughout the teaching/learning process, so as to serve as a point of reference when it comes to assessing the degree in which the desired capacities have developed.

In the *Decree 231/2002, June 6th*, the assessment criteria are established for the first year of *Bacharelato* .

The student will be able to:

*****Communicative skills.*

a. *Extract global and specific information from oral messages produced by classmates, the teacher or mass media; recognize the communicative strategies used by interlocutors and in written texts on subjects of general interest and use* *skills and strategies concerning different text types and reading purposes.*

b. *Take part in conversations or discussions on topics of interest prepared beforehand, by using appropriate strategies, and produce coherent messages and with enough formal accuracy to make communication possible.*

c. *Extract by oneself the information in different texts on up-to-date topics, on the general culture of the English-speaking countries or subjects concerning the students' interests and studies, by predicting and inferring data from context.*

d. *Write, with the help of appropriate reference material, diverse texts with enough syntactic correctness so as to be understood and use the different elements which give cohesion and coherence to the text.*

*****Reflections on language.*

a) *Reflect on the English language system by reasoning, arguing, predicting, synthesizing and inducing the corresponding rules.*

b) *Use linguistic reference items (grammatical, lexical, orthographic, phonetic and textual) which facilitate systematic learning.*

c) *Apply their knowledge of English grammar to new situations.*

d) *Use resources, sources of information and reference material autonomously to contrast conclusions, to systematize and consolidate knowledge.*

e) *Reflect on one's own learning process, by accepting and correcting mistakes, reformulating rules, expressing definitions of what has been learnt and advancing in the learning process.*

*****Socio-cultural aspects.*

a) *Interpret defining features of the culture of English-speaking countries and show knowledge of geographical, historical, artistic, literary data and incorporate this knowledge into contextualized communicative situations.*

b) *Approach the social and cultural diversity transmitted by the foreign language and look for similarities and differences between one's own culture and that of English-speaking countries.*

c) *Get to know and appreciate one's own culture better through the socio-cultural information transmitted by the foreign language.*

Taking these criteria as the closest reference, in each teaching unit more specific assessment criteria have been included, which once applied to the development activities will indicate the degree of success in reaching the teaching objectives.

WHEN TO ASSESS?

Even though assessment must be carried out throughout the teaching/learning process, we can highlight three key moments:

- At the beginning of the course and of each teaching unit, a motivating **initial assessment** will be performed so as to check the actual level of starting knowledge and be able to establish the goals or objectives to be reached. Its purpose is diagnostic or prognostic, and it marks the beginning of continuous assessment.
- During the development of the teaching units a **continuous assessment** shall be performed by means of the assessment instruments. This is a formative type of assess-

ment which provides the teacher with continued information on the teaching/learning process.

- Finally, through **final** or **summative assessment** we intend to perform a global assessment of the teaching/learning process at the end of every teaching unit, term and year. Thus, the assessment information collected through a variety of methods over a certain period of time will help the teacher to make overall judgements about the students.

HOW TO ASSESS?

When determining "how to assess" we must talk about **assessment procedures** (methods, techniques or strategies used in the carrying out of the assessment process) and **assessment instruments** (the specific resource used to gather information). Taking into account that assessment must be global, ample and continuous, it is logical to say that it must be flexible and diverse, both in its procedures and in its instruments.

With the aim of determining the starting knowledge of the students, they will fill in an **initial assessment test**. This instrument will be resorted to again informally (by asking questions to the class) at the beginning of each of the teaching units.

I will now enumerate the follow-up assessment instruments:

1. Direct and systematic observation of work performed in the classroom (attention paid, interest shown, questions asked, following work procedures, respect for rules, cooperation and team work...). The most characteristic instruments of observation are *scales of observation, class registers and a class diary.*

2. Task assessment performed by students (both in class and at home) allows us to know how they apply the contents learned as well as to notice their progress and difficulties.

3. Formal (oral and written) testing: it helps check acquisition of contents and proper reasoning. In each term there will be one written test and a global assessment exam at the end. I enclose an oral exam correction criteria sheet as well.

4. Interviews and questionnaires. Thanks to the students' answers we may evaluate their interests and opinions, their background, their relations within the class or their self-esteem as students.

5. Co-evaluation and self-evaluation. (or peer-assessment/self-assessment) Though done by using some of the already mentioned instruments, they have the peculiarity that they are done by students themselves, either individually (in self-evaluation) or among themselves and evaluating each other (in co-evaluation). Comparing the teacher's opinion with those of the students is a positive measure since it may help to modify previous ideas of the teacher with respect to the students and to make the student have a more adjusted concept of himself/herself.

******Grading criteria.** In order to quantify thc results obtained during the educational process, it is necessary to ponder the assessment instruments so as to be able to prepare suitable retaking procedures. With this in mind, the following grading criteria have been established:

A) Concepts and procedures: **90%**

A.1 1st and 2nd Trimester Tests (T1 & T2) and Final Test (FT):

(T1 & T2) → 40% ; (FT) → 30%

A.2 Continuous assessment follow-up: 20%

B) Attitudes: **10%**

******Retaking procedures.** With the purpose of easing the retaking process for those students who do not attain the minimum objectives for each term, they will receive a bulletin of activities as guidance in order to pass the term and catch up with the rest of the group. This bulletin of exercises shall be handed in before the make-up exam in June.
Students who have not passed the term in June shall be given a series of activities to be done during the summer and handed in September. The September make-up exam will be designed on the basis of the activities proposed in the mentioned bulletin.
The final September mark will be the average of the mark of the bulletin of completed exercises and that of the make-up exam.

Assessing the teacher and the teaching process...

Apart from asking the students' opinions about the activities both informally and through the use of questionnaires. The T/L process must be evaluated by periodical meetings of the Department. There, we must analyze the processes and results obtained in order to draw certain conclusions that lead to improved planning of future courses.
This involves two main types of action: assessment of the syllabus and its implementation, and proposals for improvement derived from that assessment.

The assessment of the syllabus must be performed by the whole department taking into account the personal experiences of all its components, as well as the results and opinions of the students reflected in the questionnaire mentioned in the point referred to assessment.
The situation must also be compared to previous terms, and views be shared among the other teachers of the same groups.

9. STRUCTURE OF THE TEACHING UNITS

This syllabus has been designed to cover the approximately 80-90 hours of class available at the level of 1st year *Bacharelato*. It contains 15 didactic units, logically and coherently sequenced. In each unit there will be a variety of activities covering the four skills, and providing a set of attractive and mainly authentic and semi-authentic material. The activities have been designed for different groupings, individually, in pairs and in groups, in order to maximize participation in class, and therefore to maximize learning. Each of the fifteen units contains material and activities for 5 to 6 classes, and a quantity of optional reinforcement and extension activities are also included, to attend to diversity. Each unit is divided into the following sections:

A) Reading

B) Grammar

C) Vocabulary

D) Computers

E) Listening

F) Pronunciation

G) Speaking

H) Writing

At the end of each unit I will include a Progress Check. Moreover, extensive reading in the form of graded readers will also be done throughout the year.

The final unit consists of revision material for the accumulative and systematic consolidation of the contents of the previous fourteen units. This final unit only contains reading and writing activities.

Now I would like to have a look at each section of my units:

A. READING: Throughout the different units students will be working with a variety of text types including newspaper and magazine articles, comics and extracts from literature. They have been carefully chosen taking into account their possible appeal to 16-to-17 year old students and deal with motivating and up-to-date topics. Each unit will begin with an introductory oral warm-up activity, which will serve to introduce the topic, engage the students' attention and revise previous knowledge. The main objective of my reading activities is improving reading and getting students to become good readers. What is a good reader? A good reader can read quickly. For this reason I will be working on the sub-skills of skimming the text quickly for general information and scanning for specific information. Moreover good readers are also able to read slowly and in a detail way, understanding the text in depth. This will also be practised, providing practice of the main task types that feature in the university entrance exam, as well as offering more general comprehension work. The third feature of good readers is that they are able to use their imagination and previous experience to help them understand a text, being independent without relying on a dictionary. In order to get this I will develop the sub-skills of Inferring and predicting the meaning of unknown words using the context. Finally, at the end of each reading section pupils will engage in a discussion question, which gives pupils the chance to express their own views on the topic, and to personalize the acquired information.

B. GRAMMAR. A recent survey carried out by the government to carry out an educative reform showed that students feel more confident when learning a foreign language if they are taught grammar. In my grammar sections I will work to consolidate the grammar that students have learned in the final years of *ESO*. Moreover, I will also extend students' knowledge by focussing on new aspects of these structures. There may be some times in which a deductive teaching of grammar, that is, presenting students with the rules, is advisable. However, recent methodologies tend to advocate for an inductive method, which involves that students make out and complete the rules of use after having observed examples in context. My grammar activities will be arranged from the easiest to the most difficult activities. Moreover, there is also a balance between the more mechanical type of drill activity and more communicative grammar practice.

C. VOCABULARY. The acquisition of new vocabulary is essential in *Bacharelato*, as students are more or less familiar with almost any grammar structure and must enlarge their vocabulary to become communicatively effective. Vocabulary-learning strategies, such as using a dictionary and storing vocabulary, need to be developed. For this reason I will combine vocabulary drawn from the topic of each unit with work on word-building. Students will explore the meaning and use of vocabulary and perform controlled and more creative practice activities.

D. COMPUTERS. In each unit I will be proposing a web quest, so that students become aware of the quantity of information to which they have access in English. By means of web quests I will be highlighting the importance of significant learning, using the English language as a way of acquiring knowledge in other areas.

E. LISTENING. Listening is the best way of becoming a good speaker, as the learner is exposed to new vocabulary and structures in a real, significant context. In each unit I will be proposing a listening text related to the topic of unit. Throughout the listening students will recycle the grammar and vocabulary that was presented earlier in the unit. In the listening activities students will be practicing a range of useful listening skills, such as listening for gist and listening for specific information. Most listening activities will be followed by a discussion question in order to personalise the activity by giving students the chance to express their own views on the topic.

F. PRONUNCIATION. Student will have a question on pronunciation in their exam for university entrance, so preparation should begin as soon as possible to build up students' confidence. Pupils will be asked first to identify sound patterns. This will be followed by practice in the production of difficult sounds, intonation patterns and word and sentence stress.

G. SPEAKING. I want to promote fluent, creative and natural conversation. Speaking tasks will be guided, giving students the opportunity to express their ideas and opinions in a clear and orderly manner. In order to achieve that, I will provide the students with useful expressions, idioms and previous practice of structures.

H. WRITING. Writing is a very difficult task for our students. For that reason the writing sections give extensive practice in all the main essay types that feature in the university entrance exam, such as opinion essays, narratives, descriptions, for and against essays, summaries and letters. Teachers need to help and guide students through the writing process until they become aware of the strategies, templates and so on they need. For that reason, the writing sections will also focus on a range of useful writing skills including work on organising ideas, linking words, useful expressions and formulae, and checking for mistakes. Students are prepared step-by-step for writing their own essays. Each section includes a model essay which is analysed, and students are given clear essay plans to help them.

I. OPTIONAL REINNFORCEMENT AND EXTENSION ACTIVITIES. We have to recognise that not all the students in a class have the same capacities and abilities, so I will provide optional activities to accompany each unit in order to cater for diversity in the classroom or to reinforce a certain teaching point. These have been selected so as to allow the students to work independently and autonomously and mostly cover the reading and writing skills.

J. ADDITIONAL EXTENSIVE READING. I would like to promote not only fluency in the reading skill but also reading for pleasure, so additional extensive reading is proposed in the form of graded readers, specially selected to attend to the likes, interests and abilities of the age-group.

K. PROGRESS CHECKS. At the end of each unit I have included a one-page progress check. Students can use the progress checks as a form of self-evaluation to assess their strengths and weaknesses and to revise their knowledge throughout the year.

www.ingramcontent.com/pod-product-compliance
Ingram Content Group UK Ltd.
Pitfield, Milton Keynes, MK11 3LW, UK
UKHW041837200726
13854UKWH00003BA/1181

9 781409 203230